Víctor Terán

POEMS
DIIDXADO'

poetry
translation
centre

First published in 2010
by The Poetry Translation Centre Ltd
PO Box 61051
London SE16 4YY

www.poetrytranslation.org

ISBN: 978-0-9560576-1-7

Thanks to the editors of the following publications, where the following poems were printed,
sometimes in slightly different forms:

ASH: 'I Woke with Your Name'
Hayden's Ferry Review: 'Whirlwind', 'I Know Your Body'
Oxford Magazine: 'Just Yesterday'
Poetry: 'The North Wind Whips'
World Literature Today: 'From the Palm of My Hand', 'Six Variations on Love', 'Your Name'

The Poetry Translation Centre gratefully acknowledges the financial support
of Arts Council England.

British Library Cataloguing-in-Publication Data.
A catalogue record for this book is available from the British Library.

Designed in Albertina by Libanus Press
and printed in Great Britain by the
MPG Books Group, Bodmin and King's Lynn

Contents

Introduction

The poetry of bathos is, for the most part, easy to translate: sentimentality is fairly simple to render into another language, because it is universally understood. What is more difficult to translate, in my experience, is poetry that toys with sentimentality without ever crossing into its territory, poetry that counterbalances abstraction with precision. And that's Víctor Terán's poetry. This particular talent is most evident in his love poems. He ends a poem about a breakup:

Though you left me, how can I abhor you?
You left me with an ocean of dazzling fish,
an ocean of incessant fish.

And in another about the beauty of his lover's body, he counters bold, almost pastoral statements with a comparison he develops through the poem:

If you were a city
I could give perfect directions
to wherever they asked me.

As in the first example, Terán often gets away with an abstract or maudlin line by deploying one of his typically fierce images in the line to follow. In his poem, 'Whirlwind', he balances the romance of his 'heart stretched across the bed, waiting', with these lines:

... the pigs make known
that they attack the boy squatting to do his business.

In Isthmus Zapotec there is a special expression reserved for missing an appointment, 'cuxhidxi tobi zinnña', which literally means that someone is rustling the leaves of the palm tree. 'Caxidxi zinnña', means 'palm leaves rustle', and it is commonly used to express the grumbling frustration of the person who waited in vain for the no-show and who, according to Zapotec tradition, has been mocked by their non-appearance. In the case of the poem, 'The North Wind Whips', the shame provoked by that missed appointment is the reason why the north wind, which usually assaults the isthmus between October and February, beats so ruthlessly on the village.

It is difficult to approach the edge of sentimentality without crossing it, and it is equally difficult to get as close to that edge as Terán has managed in Isthmus Zapotec. This funambulism is even more significant an achievement for Terán considering the state of the language: a Zapotec dialect spoken by fewer than one-hundred-thousand inhabitants of the Isthmus of Tehuantepec, in Oaxaca, Mexico. In many of the villages of Oaxaca, Spanish has already displaced Zapotec as the language of the family, although others have cloistered the language in their homes. When this stage of language attrition is reached, nostalgia-drenched poetries often writhe in overt politics or accounts of their romanticised demise. Terán's hometown of Juchitán, where the Zapotec still keep their doors open, remains a beacon of Zapotec language and culture.

The indigenous poetries of Mexico deserve more attention than that granted by the novelty of their exoticism. Of these poetries, Nahuatl poetry is probably the oldest written American poetry, recited by its *tlamatinis* (literally, 'habitual knowers of things') from pictoglyphs, 'singing the painted books', for more than 2,000 years before their colonisation by the Spanish. The Nahuatl tradition still thrives today, perhaps the largest contemporary indigenous tradition of Mexico, in both oral and written forms. Contemporary Mexico is home to over 200 living languages – including more than 50 dialects of Zapotec, many not mutually intelligible – and a wide variety of poetries. Of the Zapotec poets writing today, Terán is the most lyrical, the most assaultingly imagistic. Though his poems can be some of the most difficult to translate, they are often the most successful English renditions of the contemporary Zapotec tradition.

DAVID SHOOK

BIETE BI

Biete bi.
Lu neza gui'chi' ne bacuela
nanda saaca' ne xiana.
Ruguubeedxe' ca yoo, ridopa cuuxhu' bi'cu'.
Daabi ti xiixa
bicuininá' huadxí ri',
ti guichi guluxu,
ti guiiba' tini.

Nuu tu laa
gudu'ba' xhaata' gueza guibá',
bisaana ni naté, nagu'xhu'.
Xaguete' ri' guiruti'
nibeezá xpandá',
guirá' zeguyoo ra lidxi
cugaba' xquenda zí'.

Caxidxi zinña,
laaca tuuxa biaanatá'
gudxite xcunaa laa.
Yanadxí guirá'
bietenala'dxi' ladeñee,
málasi gunna binni
nabani guendaruseegu' ra lidxi.

Tu laa nanna
xiñee cazaaca' huadxí ri',
xiñee nisi nuaa'
gudxiga' yaana' xii
bixé' cundubi rarí'.

THE NORTH WIND WHIPS

The north wind whips through,
in the streets papers and leaves
are chased with resentment.
Houses moan,
dogs curl into balls.
There is something in the afternoon's finger,
a catfish spine,
a rusty nail.

Someone unthinkingly
smoked cigarettes in heaven,
left it overcast, listless.
Here, at ground level, no one could
take their shadow for a walk,
sheltered in their houses, people
are surprised to discover their misery.

Someone didn't show,
their host was insulted.
Today the world
agreed to open her thighs,
suddenly the village comprehends
that it is sometimes necessary to close their doors.

Who can divine
why I meditate on this afternoon?
Why is it birthed in me
to knife the heart
of who uncovered the mouth
of the now whipping wind,
to jam corncobs in the nose
of the ghost that pants outside?

Cuxidxi ca yaga,
riaba riásaca'
cuxidxica' naa
runi biaanata'ya'.

Latané naa nagasi
guirá' manihuiini' ruunda'
guidxélatu lu yaga,
ti gabe' laatu
pa naye'que' guichalaga binidxaba'.

The trees roar with laughter,
they split their sides,
they celebrate
that you haven't arrived at your appointment.

Now bring me
the birds
that you find in the trees,
so I can tell them
if the devil's eyelashes are curled.

XHOOPA' DIIDXA' RUI' XIINGA GUENDARANAXHII

I

Guendaranaxhii
zeedayaca casi ti xiixa nanaa
ni qui zanda guá' binni xadxí
ne qui quiba' dí ra yanni.

II

Guendaranaxhii
zeedayaca casi ti lúdxibele ruaa gui'ri',
casi gubidxa rihuinni guibá',
zadu'yanu ziyuí', málasi guibani,
zadu'yanu zié ne zeeda.

III

Guendaranaxhii
dxiña yaga nga laa,
niidxi zee guladi' telayú,
niidxi zee ruxooñe'
lade le' xtí' ti gunaa.

IV

Guie' du'ga' nga guendaranaxhii,
xquenda guchachi', ná' ti bidó'.
Zánnanu cusiabirí ladxido'no
ne qui zadu'yadi'nu laa.

SIX VARIATIONS ON LOVE

I

Love
comes along like an onerous bundle
that cannot be carried for long
without ending in cursing.

II

Love
comes along like a candle flame
or like the sun that shines in the sky:
we watch it falter, later flare up
we watch its birth, to return another day.

III

Love
is wild honey that seeps from a tree,
sap of tender maize-cob generous at dawn,
sap that runs
through the intimate garden of a woman.

IV

The flower of the fig tree is love.
The iguana trickster or hand of a goddess,
it announces its presence to the heart
but we never see it.

V

Guendaranaxhii
rie ne reeda casi huaxhinni.
Ni rie, riné ti ndaa ladxido'no,
ni reeda, reedacaa xtindaa
lu ni biaana.

VI

Guendaranaxhii
qui gapa xiladxi'
casi guendahuará,
qui gapa guendabiaani'
casi guendaguti.

V

Love
goes and comes like the night.
When it goes it flees with a slice of the soul.
When it comes it ransacks
what's left of the heart.

VI

Love
blooms without losing sleep
like illness
it doesn't understand worries
like death.

YUDÉ CUYAA

Yudé cuyaa galaabato' ná' tapa neza.
Ca yaga nagá' caguíteca' tu jmá naguudxi deche.
Ladxiduá' nexhegaa lu luuna' cabeza lii. Bezaluá' zuba,
rinaaze' bi guichaíque, zuba, cugaba' panda bihui
culaa xii ti xcuidi zubaxuuna'.

Laga lii ya', xi cayuni ndou' nagasi.
Nannu' xiinga guendaribeza ti gunaa
gueeda guxhídxiná'
lu gande iza xtí' ti badunguiiu la?

Yudé cuyaa galaabato' bizaluá'.
Ti mani' canareeguite ndaani' ca nezarini xtinne'.
Gunaa bazeendu', xi binidxaba' cayu'nu' qui gueedu'.
Ma' bigaba' birá bicuininá' gubidxa,
bi yooxho' ma' bigani lu neza, bidxaga ruaa,
cachuundu', ma' nacahui guibá',
ndaani' naya' nexheguundu' guguhuiini'
guleza lii.

WHIRLWIND

The dust dances in the middle of the path.
The leafy trees compete to make the most elegant curtsies.
My heart stretched across the bed, waiting for you. Quiet eyes,
the air tangles your hair, quiet, the pigs make known
that they attack the boy squatting to do his business.

And you, what would you be doing in this instant.
Do you, by chance, know what it is to wait for a woman
who comes to touch
the twenty waiting years of a man?

The dust dances in the eclipse of my eyes.
A chestnut fizzes through the paths of my blood.
Perverse woman, where the hell are you, what the hell are you doing.
I've already counted each of the sun's fingers,
the wind's gust quit exciting the street, silenced by fatigue.
It is twilight, the sky is filled with shadows,
in my hands it lies dying,
the turtledove that dreamed of cooing you to sleep.

NEEGUE' CA

Neegue' ca nga
sica ti xcuidi
nacu ti neza lari cubi[2]
xquendaranaxhiee'.

Neegue' ca nga
rilué' xquiibalé yu'du'
ze' ne zeeda
cabidxi yeche' mixa'.

Yanna nuaa'
sica ti binidxaapa' bida'na'[3]
ne qui nuxooñenécabe laa,
sica ti gubidxa bidé xiaga
ni gatigá rindisa bi
rucheeche laa.

JUST YESTERDAY

Just yesterday
my love was
like a kid breaking in
the year's new clothes.

Just yesterday
I was a bell
joyfully coming and going
announcing mass.

Now I am
like the virgin bride whose lover
refused consummation,
like a sun finished burning
whose ash
            is scattered by the wind.

NDAANI' BATANAYA'

Ndaani' batanaya'
cayó huadxí ri':
mani' té bilaa runi ma' bio'xho',
mani' guude, mani' biidi'.

Nexhe' ti neza lase'
deche dani rihuinni rarica',
lubí chonna bayu' quichi'
ruluí' zeca', zeca'
cuzabinaca' luá'.
Nugaanda guendaribana'
xquixhe ndaani' ladxiduá',
ne guendananala'dxi'
cutuxhu lugu' xquiiba'.

Rietetí layú rarí',
layú guichi, layú guie.
Guxhu' ne za rihuinni,
za, gu'xhu' ne guendananá.

Neza lase' ziyeeque'
deche dani rica',
neza lase' riné ra lídxilu'.
Za yu'la' biaa guibá' ca la?
zándaca cayuuyu' ní,
zándaca cayuuyu' ní,
cadi bia' za ca nga xquendaranaxhiee',
cadi bia' za ca.

FROM THE PALM OF MY HAND

From the palm of my hand
the afternoon eats its meal:
lean horse abandoned for being old,
nagging horse, dirty horse.

There is a trail
behind the hill
you see there.
In the open sky
three white tissues distance themselves,
saying goodbye.
Nostalgia has hung
its hammock in my heart
and my grudges
hastily sharpen their weapons.

Here the earth is broken,
land of acacias and stones.
In the sky smoke and clouds are visible,
clouds, smoke, and grief.

The footpath that zigzags
behind that slope
leads to your house.
The long cloud that extends across the horizon—
maybe you are looking at it,
maybe you look at it now.
My love for you is not the size of that cloud,
not that size.

Nutaabi yuuba' guendarietenala'dxi' ladxiduá'
cue' lindaa huadxí te di'.
Nuu tu zuba caguiba xquendanayeche'
xa'na' yaga baca'nda' xti' ti guendaranaxhii la?
Guidxilayú ri' naca ti dxia naro'ba' qui gapa xhibia'
candaabi' lu xté diuxi.
Binidxaba' canaguyaa lu neza
laga ti bi'cu' nagola
zixupila'na' xcuaana' gundagaa guete'.

Gudaabi' ladxiduá' bi sisi,
gudaa ti bacaanda' do' ndaani' ca bezaluá',
ti bacaanda' do' ziuula' sica ziuula' guendaguti.

Rietenala'dxe' ca bicuininá' be,
ca bicuininá' lase' be.
Rabixhinni bezaluá' runi ca beeu guidiruaa be.
Nutaabi xhiuuba' be naa cué' huadxí yanda di'
ne rilué' xpandá' ti gue'tu' bigaachi' neegue',
bandá' ruyadxi guiá', ruyadxi guete',
nisi bieque rudii ra zuhuaa.

Nabani guendarusiaanda'.
Zándaca runi nga diuxi qui huayati.
Tuungue ná,
pa sou' lu gui
zazou' lu bi, que?

YOUR MEMORY

Nostalgia has me boxed
in the stupid wall of this afternoon.
Someone somewhere bastes in happiness
beneath the fresh shade of love.
The earth is like a great *comal*[1]
above God's hot coals.
Gnomes hop across red-hot paths
while a dog
compulsively licks her vulva, then wanders southward.

Console my soul, clumsy air,
spill into my eyes the deepest dream,
a dense dream and distant like death.

I recall the fingers of your hand,
your bony fingers.
My eyes choke for the moons of your lips.
Your memory has me nailed to the lukewarm afternoon
and I resemble the shadow of a body buried yesterday,
a shadow that looks to the north, to the south,
that seeks, without finding, the path.

Forgetting exists.
Maybe because of this, God doesn't die.
Who said
that if someone can walk over coals
they can also do it over the wind?

1 A *comal* is a type of skillet for cooking tortillas and other indigenous
staples. Originating in pre-Colombian times, it comes from the Nahuatl
word *comalli*, and is made of cast iron or, more commonly in indigenous
communities, flattened scrap metal.

Bixidxila' gúdxibe naa
laga cutaabi be guiiba' diidxa'
Sicarú guyé ti'xhi' xquendaranaxhiee',
laga cayabi be naa   *Ma' qui zadu'yanu* .

Bixidxi la' bandá'
pacaa guyé yeyubi dxitaládilu'.

Nanda reza larindxó'
guendarietenala'dxi' xtinne' lu doo
runi bi yooxho' guidiruaa be.

Laugh at me please, you told me
while the fierce metal of the phrase
I wish you all the best sunk into the pit of my love,
while you told me *we won't see each other anymore.*

Laugh shadow
or beat it to look for your skeleton!

The meat of my memories
hangs in strips at the grocer's
because of the blind wind of your lips.

QUI ZUNIHUARÁ LU' NAA

Qui zunihuará lu' naa.
Qui zaguza diou' xquendanabane'.
Naro'ba' yu'du' biaani' bisaana nelu' naa,
nanaadxi' ne nayeche'.

Xadxí pe' bisindá'naxhilu' bi stinne',
xadxípe' guleezalu' naa lade ca za
ne xidxaa guidiládilu'.

Racaditi ru' ca naya' guietenala'dxica'
beelaxiaa dxitaxa'nalu'.
Ricaala'dxiru' guidiruaa'
runi guiropa' rii dxiñabizu xi'dxu'.

Paraa chiguniná guendarietenala'dxi' naa ya'.
Paraa, neca zelu', gácananaladxe' lii ya'.
Ti nisadó' benda riaquibiaani' bisaana nelu' naa,
ti nisadó' benda caguite yeche'.

YOU WILL NOT MANAGE TO HURT ME

You will not manage to hurt me.
You will not break my existence.
The cathedral of light that you left me is immense,
warm and joyful.

You scented my existence for a long time.
You introduced me to paradise
with your lukewarm and naked body.

My hands still shake at the memory
of your fleshy ass.
My lips still tremble
when I remember the taste of your nipples.

With these memories, how can I feel hurt?
Though you left me, how can I abhor you?
You left me with an ocean of dazzling fish,
an ocean of incessant fish.

GUIDÚBILU' RUNEBIA'YA'

Guidúbilu' runebia'ya',
guidúbinaca peou'.
Pa ñácalu' ti guidxi
ratiicasi ninabadiidxa' cabe náa
naa nulué' pa neza riaana ní.
Riuuládxepea' guidúbilu',
riuuladxe' guuya' guiní'lu', guxídxilu',
guzeque yannilu'. Dxiña yaga guiropa' dani
zuguaa ndí' xtilu', ra guyaa' dxiqué
rigucaa' ruaa bidó'. Ñacaladxe' rua'
ñuá' ne niree ndaani' guixhidó' xtilu',
ni guya' dxiiña' guiluxe guendanabani ndaani'.
Biza'naadxi' bido' guzana lii, qui gápalu'
ra guidiiñeyulu'. Binnindxó' nga naa
ti bibane' lii, guca' lii. Yanna ma cadi naa
ridxiiche' gudxigueta lú ca nguiiu ra zedi'dilu',
ma cadi naa racalugua' cueelu' lari.
Ti bidxiña lubí nga lii, ti balaaga' guie'
ziguite yeche' lu guiigu' ti siadó'.

Gabati' lii nou' qui ñunebia'ya', nou'
qui ñuuladxe'. Pa ñándasi ñácarua'
biaani' ruxheleruaa ruuya' ca nduni
yuxido' quichi' beelaxa'nalu'. Pa ñándasi
nibeza rua'
       ndaani' guidxi sicarú
            ni nácalu'.

I KNOW YOUR BODY

I know your body,
entirely I know you.
If you were a city
I could give perfect directions
to wherever they asked me.
I like all of your body,
I like to see you talk, laugh,
move your head. Your two well-rounded hills
are the honey of bees, where my lips celebrate to the gods.
I would have liked to continue storming your forest,
lodgings made deliberately for a nice death.
You were created with love,
your body is worthy of praise. What an honor to have lived,
to have been. I am no longer bothered
when men turn to look at you,
I am no longer impatient when you undress.
You are a stag in the air. A raft of flowers
that snakes across the river by morning.

There is no part of your body that I do not know, there is no
part that I do not like. I want to keep being
the light stunned at the look of your white
roundness of flesh. I want to keep
living
      in the beautiful city
                that you are.

BIBANENIÁ' LALU'

Bibaneniá' lalu' naga' ndaani' yanne'.
Pa niní' ca naya' ni gunié'xcaanda'
ñuuyapiá' nusabalú diuxi.
Bandaa cayuni xhiiña' lu gueela'
sica ti gubaana' biziidichaahui'.
Ne lu bi za'bi' guendaruyadxí bana' xtinne'
naaze nanda guidiruaa.

Gasti' nou' qui runebia'ya' ndaani' yoo ra nuaa'
ne zacá ladxiduá' cayacaditi
sica ti xcuidi guladxi bi'cu'.
Rahuayaa bicuininá' xquendabiaane'
ti guibani chaahui'.
Laga ti gayuaa bigose buubu
ziyásanene lu layú ladxiduá'.

Ze'gu' lu beeu huaxhinni.
Naaze guppa larigueela' yaase' xtí' guibá'.
Pa ñanna' caniéxcaanda' qui nundaa' ca nalu',
pa ñanna' zabane' niguiidxedxiiche' lii ti que ñelu'.
Rigui'ba' ti yuuba' ra yanne'
ne ricaa runi xtí' ladxiduá'.

Paraa nda' nuu ca luyaande sicarú lu' ya',
paraa nda' ca guidiruaalu'.
Biaanaru' xiixa xtinne'
ndaani' ladxidó'lo' la?
Huandí' nga ma' biaanda' lii
ni gúcanu la?

Bibaneneá' lalu' naga' ndaani' yanne'.

I WOKE WITH YOUR NAME

I woke with your name stuck in my throat.
If my hands would say what I dreamed last night
I would certainly see God lower his view.
The termite labors at night
like an experienced thief.
And in the air my languid face hangs
with a light trembling of lips.

Nothing exists in this house that I do not know
but even so my heart trembles
like a child running around with a dog.
I bite the feet of my understanding
so that its clumsiness will wake up.
Meanwhile a flock of rooks
lifts into flight, slowly, from the empty field of my soul.

It's night and the moon is covered.
The humidity suffocates the black sheet of the sky.
If I had known I was dreaming
I would not have let go of your hands.
If I had known I was dreaming
I would have hugged you strongly
so you wouldn't leave.
A pain rises up my throat
and appropriates my heart.

In what place do your large, beautiful eyes walk about,
in what place your lips.
Does anything of mine still
exist within your heart?
Is it true that you'll forget
all that we were?

I woke with your name stuck in my throat.

LÁ LU'

Ridxí' ne huaxhinni, lá lu'.
Siadó', huadxí, lu gueela',
nisi lá lu' riree xieque
ndaani' bichuga íque'
sica tuuxa zeguyoo
runi biniti guendabiaani',
nisi lá lu' riree chuuchi
lu ludxe'
sica benda ndaani' ná'
ti guuze'.

Guindisa' ti gui'chi', lá lu'.
Cuaque' ti xiixa, lá lu'.
Gabati' nalu' nuaa'
cadi daabi guichi lá lu'
íque bicuini naya'
ne ratiicasi zedide'
málasi gó la'na'
guendarietenala'dxi' lú lu'
ñee xquendanabane'.

Ma yanna nga nabaana
ne huidxe mápeca saa guidxi.
Zándaca ridxí zaxhaca la'dxi'
sá' nanda huaxhinni.
Zándaca naa guibane' ti dxi
ne guirá' ca yaya xtí' xquendagute',
zapa ruá' ti nisadó' guendaricaala'dxi'
ndaani' ladxiduá' guzeete' lá lu',
zápa' rua' neca xtuudxi huiini' bi
guzayaniá' ti dxumisú birixhiaa
gusietenala'dxi' lii guendaranaxhii stinne'
sica rusietenala'dxi' laanu ne xquendayaya
dxi ma zeedadxiña xhí nisaguié.

YOUR NAME

Day and night, your name.
In the morning, the afternoon, at dusk
only your name spins
through my head
like a man straight-jacketed
for having lost his mind;
only your name slips
over my tongue
like a fish between the hands
of a fisherman.

I lift a paper, your name.
I put something away, your name.
There is nowhere I go
that I do not have the thorn of your name
nailed to the tip of my finger
and no matter where I go,
the memory of your face silently bites
the leg of my existence.

It is time for Lent
and May's festival is near.
Perhaps the day is fed up
with chasing the night.
Maybe one day I'll wake up
to the scandal of my death;
despite it all I'll have an ocean of sighs
in my soul, to whisper your name;
I'll undoubtedly have one last breath
capable of filling a basket with winged ants
that will proclaim the love I have,
like the commotion that announces
coming rains.